LOOK INSIDE
CROSS-SECTIONS
RECORD
BREAKERS

LOOK INSIDE
CROSS-SECTIONS
RECORD
BREAKERS

ILLUSTRATED BY
CHRIS GRIGG AND KEITH HARMER

WRITTEN BY
MOIRA BUTTERFIELD

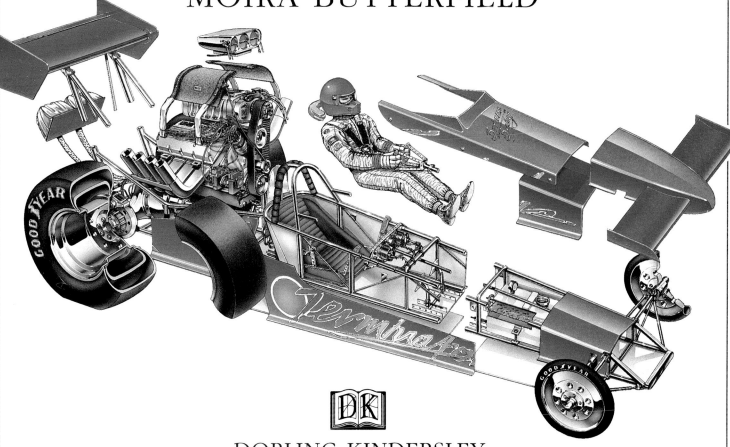

DORLING KINDERSLEY
LONDON • NEW YORK • STUTTGART

A DORLING KINDERSLEY BOOK

Art Editor Dorian Spencer Davies
Designers Sharon Grant, Sara Hill
Senior Art Editor C. David Gillingwater
Project Editor Constance Novis
Senior Editor John C. Miles
Production Louise Barratt

First published in 1995
by Dorling Kindersley Limited,
9 Henrietta Street, London WC2E 8PS

A CIP catalogue record for this book is available
from the British Library

ISBN 0-7513-5332-9

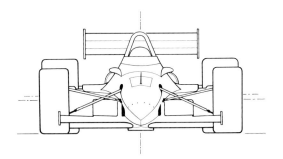

Reproduced by Dot Gradations, Essex
Printed and bound by Proost, Belgium

CONTENTS

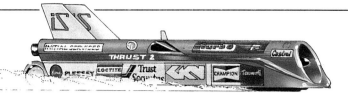

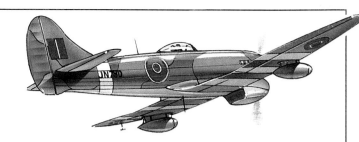

BLACKBIRD

ON 25 JULY 1964, PRESIDENT LYNDON JOHNSON

of the United States announced a new aircraft development programme. The aeroplane in question would be used for spying and reconnaissance (taking photographs of enemy territory). It would be equipped with the most sophisticated electronics and surveillance systems. It would also fly higher and faster than any other aeroplane. When the aircraft was built, it looked like nothing else in the air. Painted deep blue-black, it was officially called SR-71, although this amazing aircraft became popularly known as the "Blackbird". It still holds several air speed records today.

Speed machine
The SR-71 was designed to fly both higher and faster than any other aircraft. Its maximum speed was Mach 3.2, or more than three times the speed of sound. This is equivalent to more than 3,300 km/h (2,100 mph).

High heat
Much of the SR-71 was made of titanium, the space-age metal. Titanium is immensely strong and very resistant to the heat generated at high speeds.

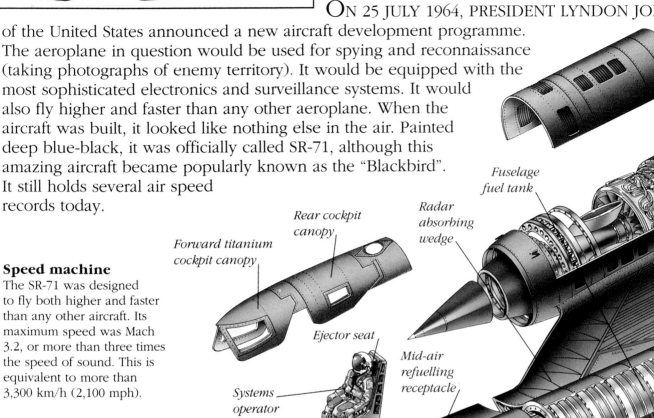

Rear cockpit canopy

Forward titanium cockpit canopy

Radar absorbing wedge

Fuselage fuel tank

Ejector seat

Systems operator

Mid-air refuelling receptacle

Rear cockpit

Pilot

Forward cockpit

Pitot tube

Technical objective camera

Electronics package

Engine inlet spike

Forward landing gear

Leading edge wing structure

Side-looking radar compartment

Liquid oxygen tank

Rear cockpit electronics

Platform computer

Environmental control system

Blackbirds
The SR-71 was painted blue-black to radiate the intense heat generated by friction (air rubbing against the aircraft) at high speed. The paint used on the SR-71 also had minute iron balls in it which helped confuse enemy radar.

Flying suits
The two-man crew of the SR-71 wore special flying suits. The suits protected them from the stresses of flying at high altitudes where the Earth's atmosphere is very thin. They also ate low-gas foods to stop them developing crippling abdominal cramps due to air pressure differences. Because the flying suits were difficult to put on, the crew "suited up" in a support van, and were driven out to the aircraft.

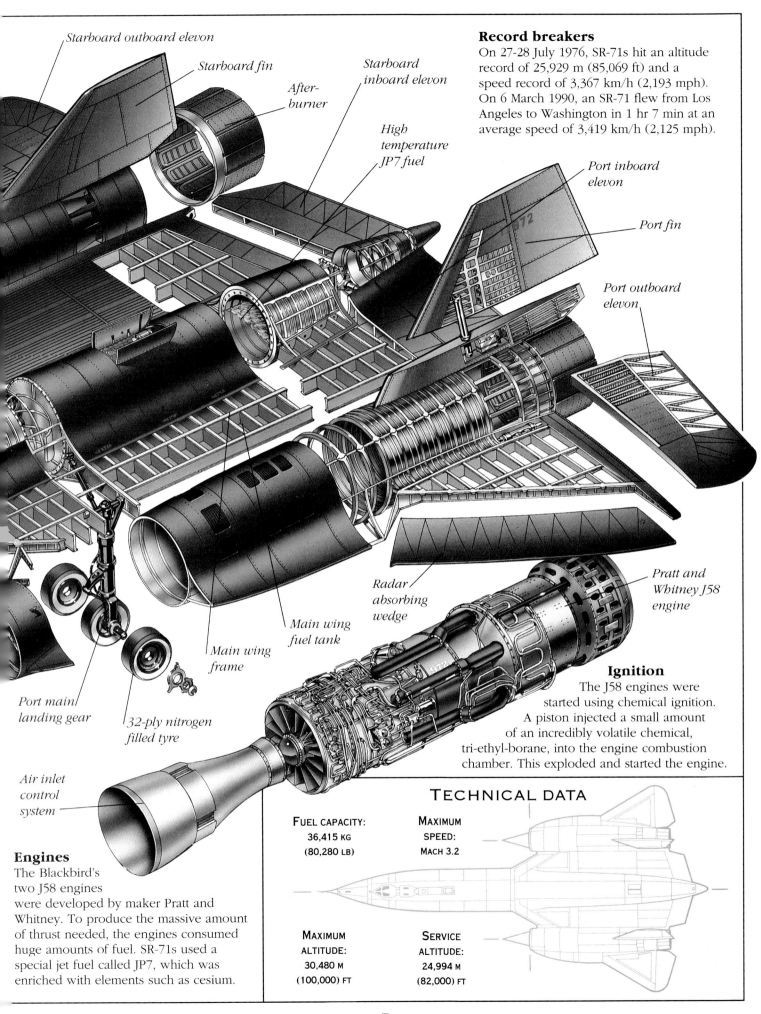

Starboard outboard elevon

Starboard fin

After-burner

Starboard inboard elevon

Starboard inboard elevon

High temperature JP7 fuel

Record breakers
On 27-28 July 1976, SR-71s hit an altitude record of 25,929 m (85,069 ft) and a speed record of 3,367 km/h (2,193 mph). On 6 March 1990, an SR-71 flew from Los Angeles to Washington in 1 hr 7 min at an average speed of 3,419 km/h (2,125 mph).

Port inboard elevon

Port fin

Port outboard elevon

Pratt and Whitney J58 engine

Radar absorbing wedge

Main wing fuel tank

Main wing frame

Port main landing gear

32-ply nitrogen filled tyre

Air inlet control system

Ignition
The J58 engines were started using chemical ignition. A piston injected a small amount of an incredibly volatile chemical, tri-ethyl-borane, into the engine combustion chamber. This exploded and started the engine.

Engines
The Blackbird's two J58 engines were developed by maker Pratt and Whitney. To produce the massive amount of thrust needed, the engines consumed huge amounts of fuel. SR-71s used a special jet fuel called JP7, which was enriched with elements such as cesium.

TECHNICAL DATA

FUEL CAPACITY:	MAXIMUM SPEED:
36,415 KG (80,280 LB)	MACH 3.2

MAXIMUM ALTITUDE:	SERVICE ALTITUDE:
30,480 M (100,000) FT	24,994 M (82,000) FT

TEA CLIPPER

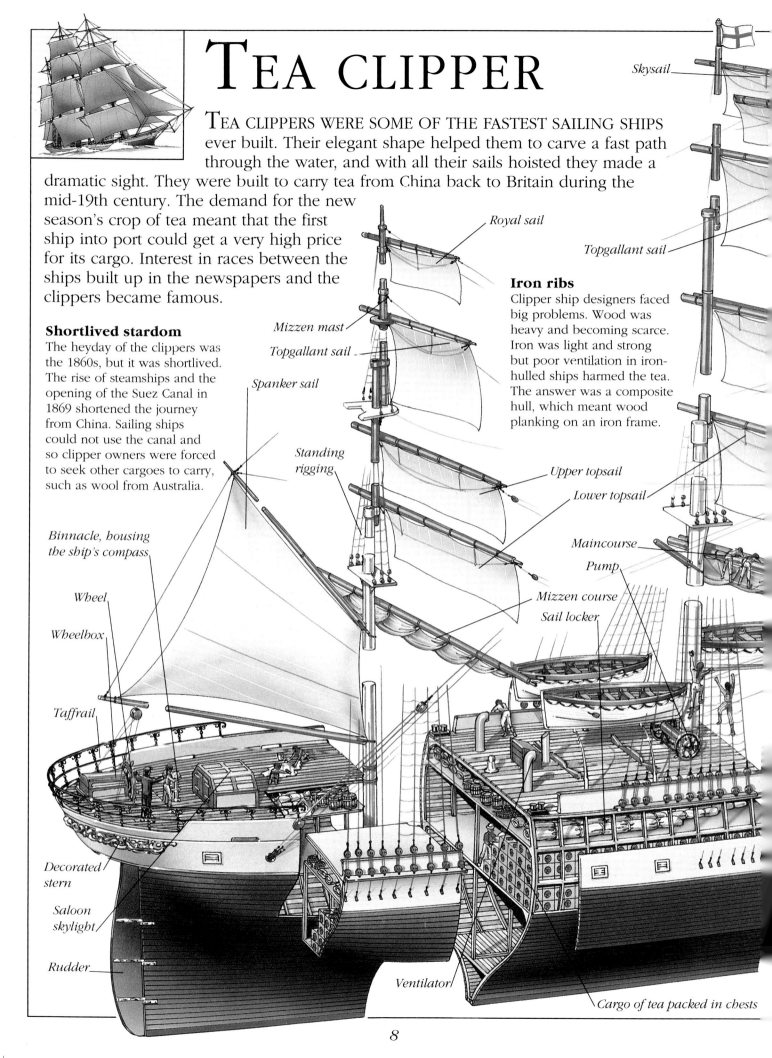

TEA CLIPPERS WERE SOME OF THE FASTEST SAILING SHIPS ever built. Their elegant shape helped them to carve a fast path through the water, and with all their sails hoisted they made a dramatic sight. They were built to carry tea from China back to Britain during the mid-19th century. The demand for the new season's crop of tea meant that the first ship into port could get a very high price for its cargo. Interest in races between the ships built up in the newspapers and the clippers became famous.

Shortlived stardom

The heyday of the clippers was the 1860s, but it was shortlived. The rise of steamships and the opening of the Suez Canal in 1869 shortened the journey from China. Sailing ships could not use the canal and so clipper owners were forced to seek other cargoes to carry, such as wool from Australia.

Iron ribs

Clipper ship designers faced big problems. Wood was heavy and becoming scarce. Iron was light and strong but poor ventilation in iron-hulled ships harmed the tea. The answer was a composite hull, which meant wood planking on an iron frame.

Skysail

Topgallant sail

Royal sail

Mizzen mast

Topgallant sail

Spanker sail

Standing rigging

Upper topsail

Lower topsail

Binnacle, housing the ship's compass

Maincourse

Pump

Wheel

Mizzen course

Sail locker

Wheelbox

Taffrail

Decorated stern

Saloon skylight

Rudder

Ventilator

Cargo of tea packed in chests

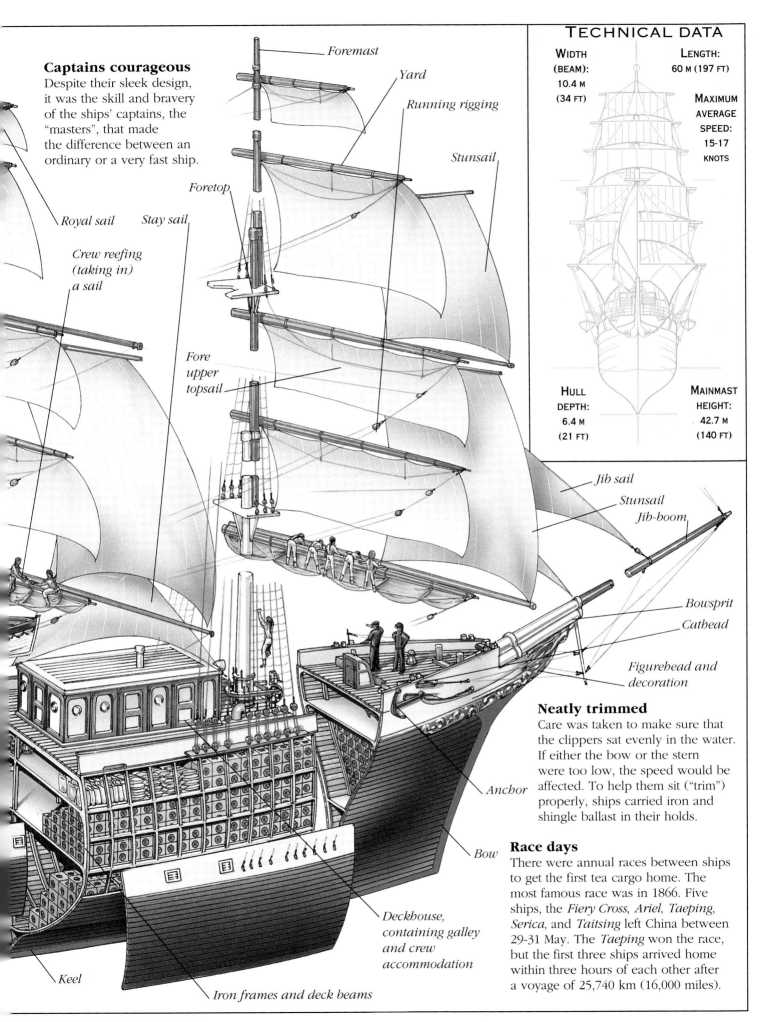

Captains courageous
Despite their sleek design, it was the skill and bravery of the ships' captains, the "masters", that made the difference between an ordinary or a very fast ship.

Foremast

Yard

Running rigging

Stunsail

Royal sail

Stay sail

Foretop

Crew reefing (taking in) a sail

Fore upper topsail

Jib sail

Stunsail

Jib-boom

Bowsprit

Cathead

Figurehead and decoration

Anchor

Bow

Deckhouse, containing galley and crew accommodation

Iron frames and deck beams

Keel

TECHNICAL DATA

WIDTH (BEAM): 10.4 M (34 FT)	LENGTH: 60 M (197 FT)
	MAXIMUM AVERAGE SPEED: 15-17 KNOTS
HULL DEPTH: 6.4 M (21 FT)	MAINMAST HEIGHT: 42.7 M (140 FT)

Neatly trimmed
Care was taken to make sure that the clippers sat evenly in the water. If either the bow or the stern were too low, the speed would be affected. To help them sit ("trim") properly, ships carried iron and shingle ballast in their holds.

Race days
There were annual races between ships to get the first tea cargo home. The most famous race was in 1866. Five ships, the *Fiery Cross*, *Ariel*, *Taeping*, *Serica*, and *Taitsing* left China between 29-31 May. The *Taeping* won the race, but the first three ships arrived home within three hours of each other after a voyage of 25,740 km (16,000 miles).

DRAGSTER

THE RACE IS ABOUT TO BEGIN AND TWO LONG, LEAN dragster cars edge forward to the start line. The lights turn to green and the cars leap away in a cloud of tyre smoke. Top Fuel dragsters, such as the one shown, are fast accelerators – the record time is 4.726 seconds to cover a quarter mile (402 m). At the end of this run the car's speed was 496.7 km/h (308.64 mph)!

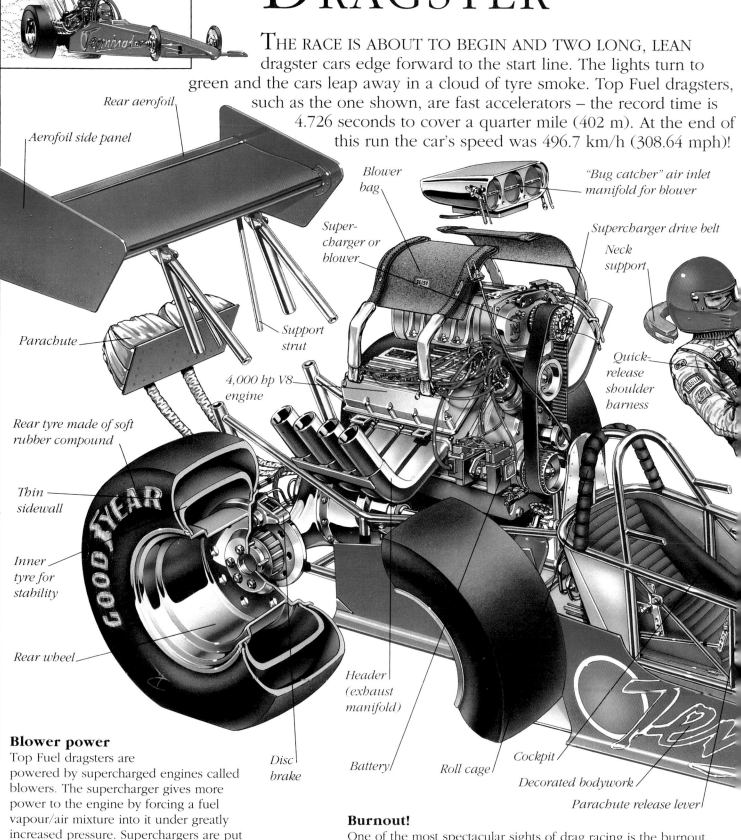

Rear aerofoil

Aerofoil side panel

Blower bag

"Bug catcher" air inlet manifold for blower

Super-charger or blower

Supercharger drive belt

Neck support

Parachute

Support strut

4,000 hp V8 engine

Quick-release shoulder harness

Rear tyre made of soft rubber compound

Thin sidewall

Inner tyre for stability

Rear wheel

Header (exhaust manifold)

Disc brake

Battery

Roll cage

Cockpit

Decorated bodywork

Parachute release lever

Blower power

Top Fuel dragsters are powered by supercharged engines called blowers. The supercharger gives more power to the engine by forcing a fuel vapour/air mixture into it under greatly increased pressure. Superchargers are put under such strain that occasionally they blow up! To avoid the danger from flying shrapnel, "blower bags", made from similar material to flak jackets, are strapped over the top of the supercharger.

Burnout!

One of the most spectacular sights of drag racing is the burnout. As part of the pre-race preparations the rear tyres are lubricated with water and made to spin very quickly. This cleans and heats them to melting point, making them very sticky. It also lays a carpet of rubber across the starting line. All this helps the dragster gain extra grip for the crucial fast start.

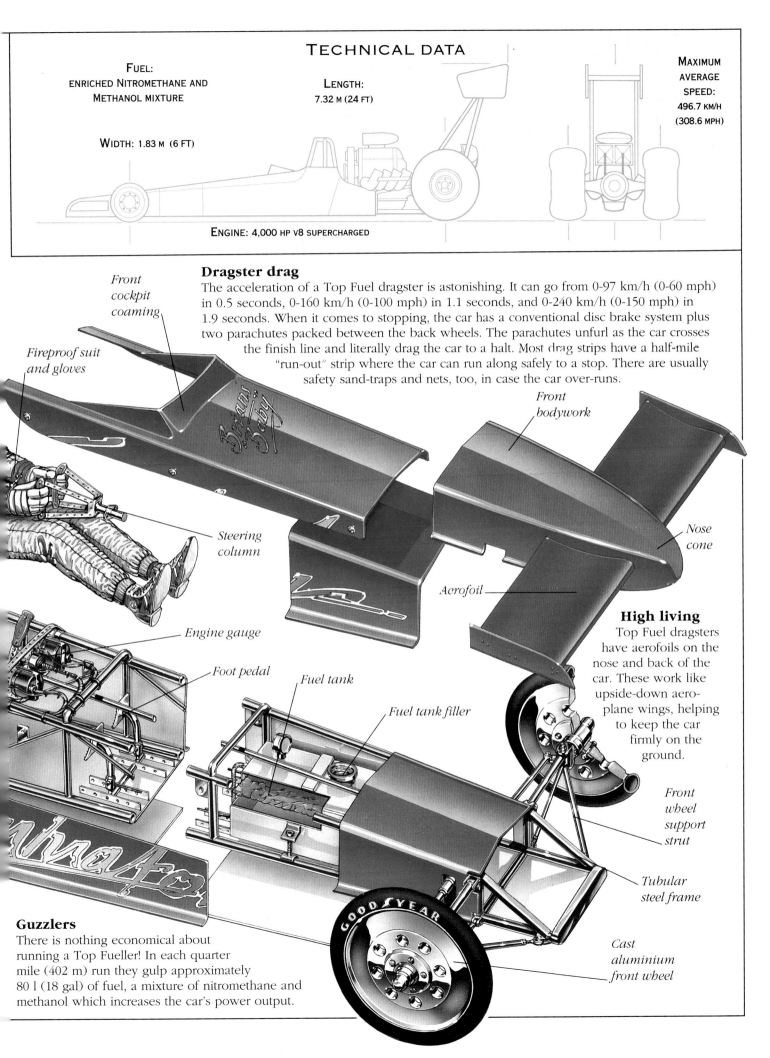

TECHNICAL DATA

FUEL:
ENRICHED NITROMETHANE AND
METHANOL MIXTURE

LENGTH:
7.32 M (24 FT)

MAXIMUM AVERAGE SPEED:
496.7 KM/H
(308.6 MPH)

WIDTH: 1.83 M (6 FT)

ENGINE: 4,000 HP V8 SUPERCHARGED

Front cockpit coaming

Fireproof suit and gloves

Dragster drag

The acceleration of a Top Fuel dragster is astonishing. It can go from 0-97 km/h (0-60 mph) in 0.5 seconds, 0-160 km/h (0-100 mph) in 1.1 seconds, and 0-240 km/h (0-150 mph) in 1.9 seconds. When it comes to stopping, the car has a conventional disc brake system plus two parachutes packed between the back wheels. The parachutes unfurl as the car crosses the finish line and literally drag the car to a halt. Most drag strips have a half-mile "run-out" strip where the car can run along safely to a stop. There are usually safety sand-traps and nets, too, in case the car over-runs.

Front bodywork

Nose cone

Steering column

Aerofoil

High living

Top Fuel dragsters have aerofoils on the nose and back of the car. These work like upside-down aeroplane wings, helping to keep the car firmly on the ground.

Engine gauge

Foot pedal

Fuel tank

Fuel tank filler

Front wheel support strut

Tubular steel frame

Guzzlers

There is nothing economical about running a Top Fueller! In each quarter mile (402 m) run they gulp approximately 80 l (18 gal) of fuel, a mixture of nitromethane and methanol which increases the car's power output.

Cast aluminium front wheel

WATER BIKE

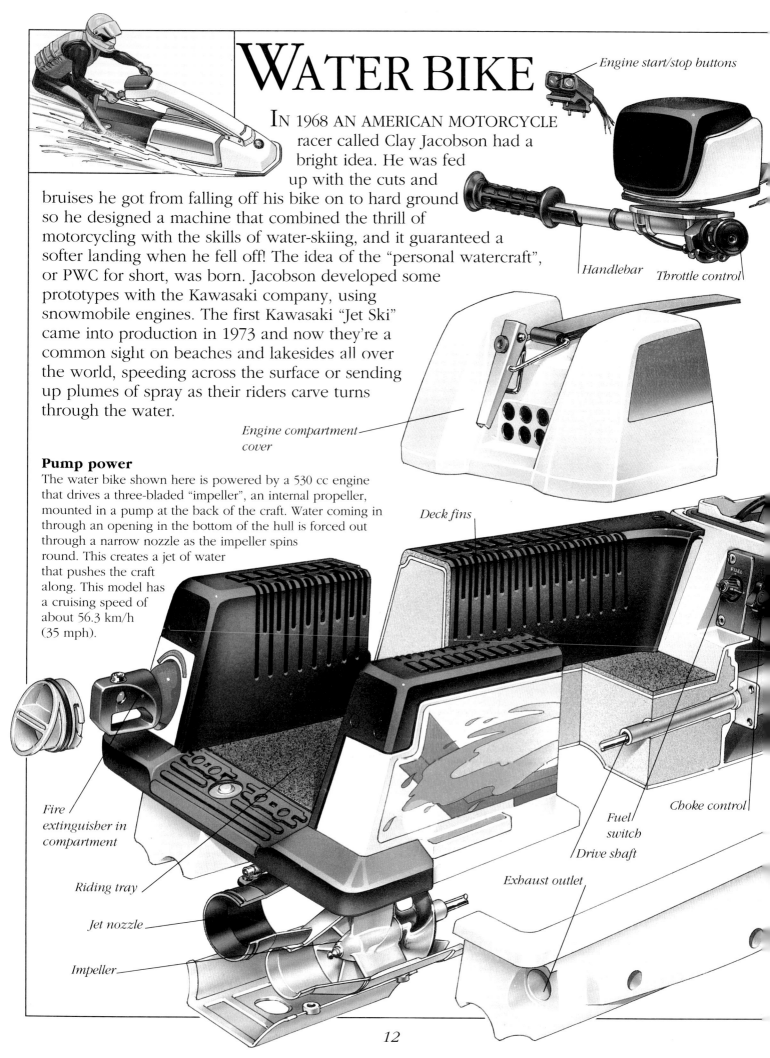

Engine start/stop buttons

IN 1968 AN AMERICAN MOTORCYCLE racer called Clay Jacobson had a bright idea. He was fed up with the cuts and bruises he got from falling off his bike on to hard ground so he designed a machine that combined the thrill of motorcycling with the skills of water-skiing, and it guaranteed a softer landing when he fell off! The idea of the "personal watercraft", or PWC for short, was born. Jacobson developed some prototypes with the Kawasaki company, using snowmobile engines. The first Kawasaki "Jet Ski" came into production in 1973 and now they're a common sight on beaches and lakesides all over the world, speeding across the surface or sending up plumes of spray as their riders carve turns through the water.

Handlebar *Throttle control*

Engine compartment cover

Pump power

The water bike shown here is powered by a 530 cc engine that drives a three-bladed "impeller", an internal propeller, mounted in a pump at the back of the craft. Water coming in through an opening in the bottom of the hull is forced out through a narrow nozzle as the impeller spins round. This creates a jet of water that pushes the craft along. This model has a cruising speed of about 56.3 km/h (35 mph).

Deck fins

Fire extinguisher in compartment

Riding tray

Jet nozzle

Impeller

Choke control

Fuel switch

Drive shaft

Exhaust outlet

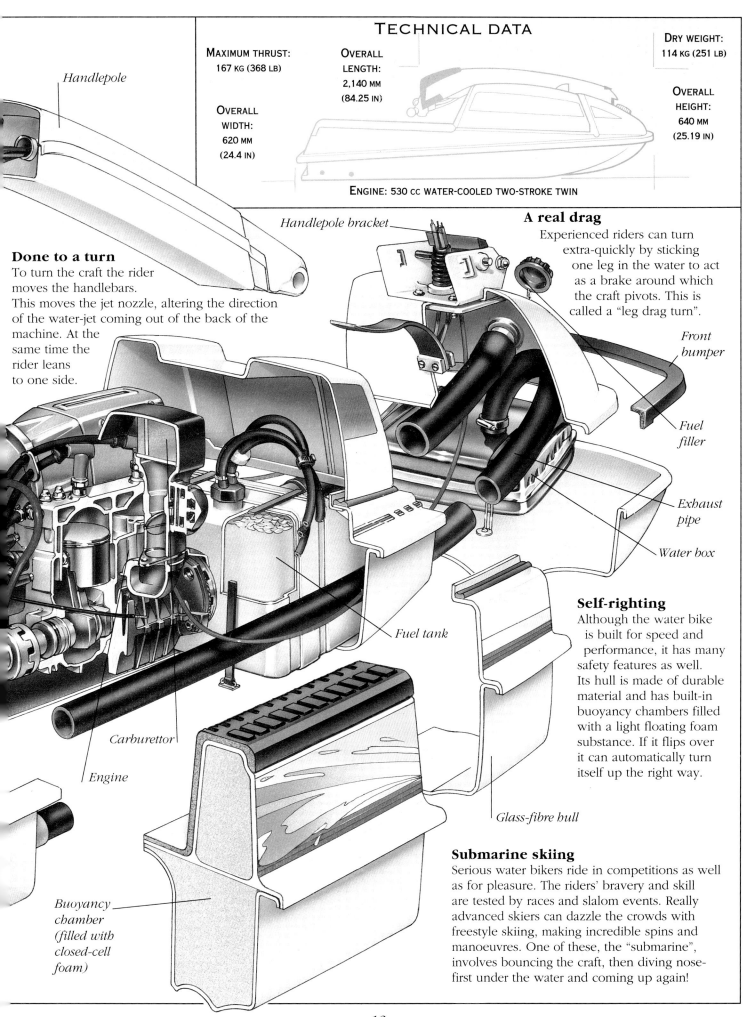

Handlepole

| MAXIMUM THRUST: | OVERALL LENGTH: | DRY WEIGHT: |
| 167 KG (368 LB) | 2,140 MM (84.25 IN) | 114 KG (251 LB) |

OVERALL WIDTH:
620 MM
(24.4 IN)

OVERALL HEIGHT:
640 MM
(25.19 IN)

ENGINE: 530 CC WATER-COOLED TWO-STROKE TWIN

Handlepole bracket

Done to a turn
To turn the craft the rider moves the handlebars. This moves the jet nozzle, altering the direction of the water-jet coming out of the back of the machine. At the same time the rider leans to one side.

A real drag
Experienced riders can turn extra-quickly by sticking one leg in the water to act as a brake around which the craft pivots. This is called a "leg drag turn".

Front bumper

Fuel filler

Exhaust pipe

Water box

Fuel tank

Carburettor

Engine

Self-righting
Although the water bike is built for speed and performance, it has many safety features as well. Its hull is made of durable material and has built-in buoyancy chambers filled with a light floating foam substance. If it flips over it can automatically turn itself up the right way.

Glass-fibre hull

Buoyancy chamber (filled with closed-cell foam)

Submarine skiing
Serious water bikers ride in competitions as well as for pleasure. The riders' bravery and skill are tested by races and slalom events. Really advanced skiers can dazzle the crowds with freestyle skiing, making incredible spins and manoeuvres. One of these, the "submarine", involves bouncing the craft, then diving nose-first under the water and coming up again!

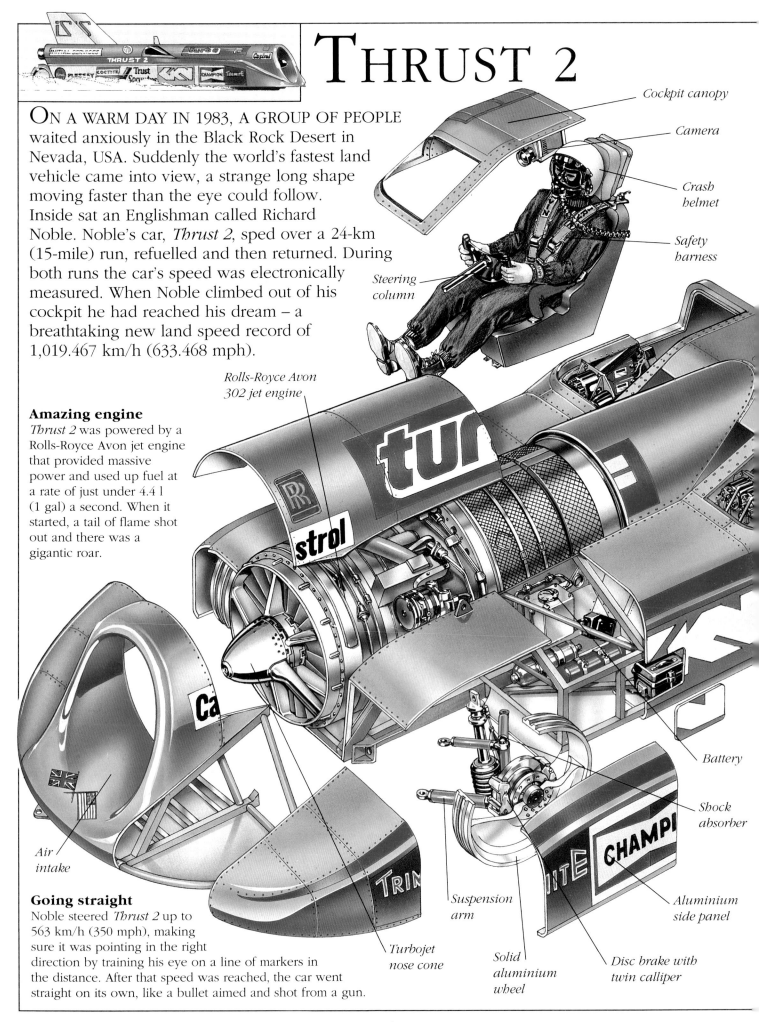

THRUST 2

ON A WARM DAY IN 1983, A GROUP OF PEOPLE waited anxiously in the Black Rock Desert in Nevada, USA. Suddenly the world's fastest land vehicle came into view, a strange long shape moving faster than the eye could follow. Inside sat an Englishman called Richard Noble. Noble's car, *Thrust 2*, sped over a 24-km (15-mile) run, refuelled and then returned. During both runs the car's speed was electronically measured. When Noble climbed out of his cockpit he had reached his dream – a breathtaking new land speed record of 1,019.467 km/h (633.468 mph).

Amazing engine

Thrust 2 was powered by a Rolls-Royce Avon jet engine that provided massive power and used up fuel at a rate of just under 4.4 l (1 gal) a second. When it started, a tail of flame shot out and there was a gigantic roar.

Going straight

Noble steered *Thrust 2* up to 563 km/h (350 mph), making sure it was pointing in the right direction by training his eye on a line of markers in the distance. After that speed was reached, the car went straight on its own, like a bullet aimed and shot from a gun.

Cockpit canopy

Camera

Crash helmet

Safety harness

Steering column

Rolls-Royce Avon 302 jet engine

Battery

Shock absorber

Air intake

Aluminium side panel

Suspension arm

Turbojet nose cone

Solid aluminium wheel

Disc brake with twin calliper

Smooth and speedy

The car's shape was long, narrow and curved to cut through the air easily at a low supersonic speed. It was carefully designed using wind tunnels and computer simulations to predict how it would act, and before the run it was polished to make it extra-smooth.

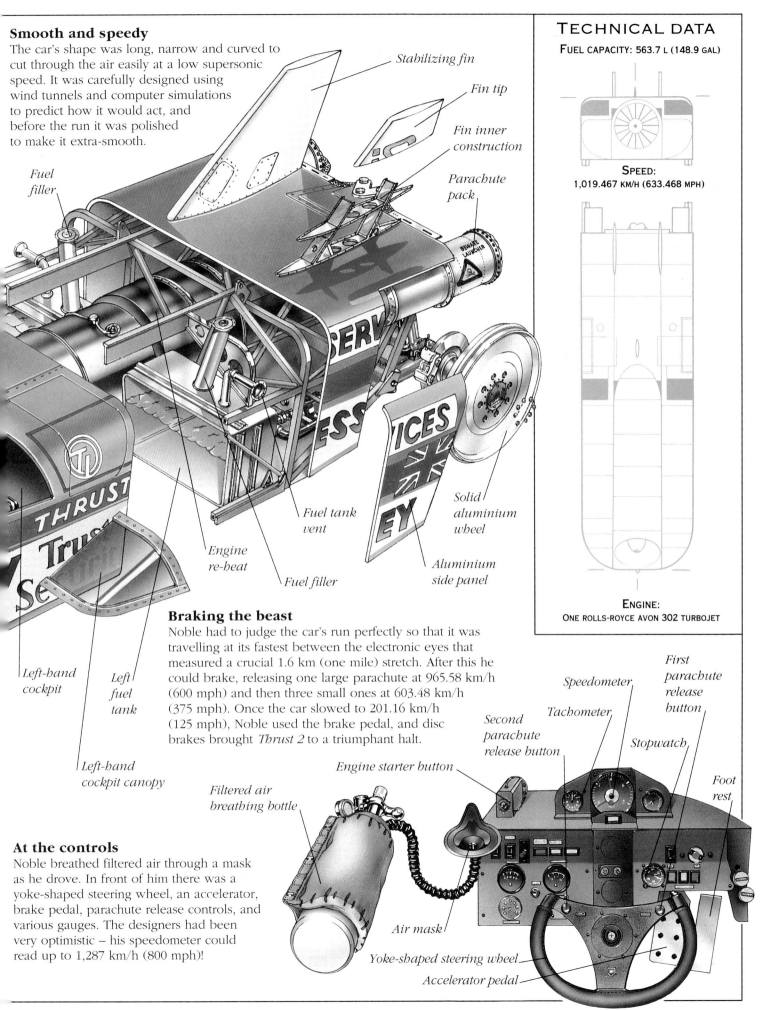

Stabilizing fin

Fin tip

Fin inner construction

Parachute pack

Fuel filler

Fuel tank vent

Engine re-heat

Fuel filler

Solid aluminium wheel

Aluminium side panel

Left-hand cockpit

Left fuel tank

Left-hand cockpit canopy

TECHNICAL DATA

FUEL CAPACITY: 563.7 L (148.9 GAL)

SPEED:
1,019.467 KM/H (633.468 MPH)

ENGINE:
ONE ROLLS-ROYCE AVON 302 TURBOJET

Braking the beast

Noble had to judge the car's run perfectly so that it was travelling at its fastest between the electronic eyes that measured a crucial 1.6 km (one mile) stretch. After this he could brake, releasing one large parachute at 965.58 km/h (600 mph) and then three small ones at 603.48 km/h (375 mph). Once the car slowed to 201.16 km/h (125 mph), Noble used the brake pedal, and disc brakes brought *Thrust 2* to a triumphant halt.

At the controls

Noble breathed filtered air through a mask as he drove. In front of him there was a yoke-shaped steering wheel, an accelerator, brake pedal, parachute release controls, and various gauges. The designers had been very optimistic – his speedometer could read up to 1,287 km/h (800 mph)!

First parachute release button

Speedometer

Tachometer

Stopwatch

Second parachute release button

Foot rest

Engine starter button

Filtered air breathing bottle

Air mask

Yoke-shaped steering wheel

Accelerator pedal

MALLARD

IMAGINE YOU'RE SITTING BY A STRETCH OF BRITAIN'S London and North Eastern Railway on a summer's day. It is 3 July 1938. Suddenly a train pulled by a sleek blue locomotive streaks by, moving faster than anything you have ever seen on rails! The engine, number 4468, is named *Mallard*, and has just set a world speed record of 202 km/h (126 mph) for steam locomotives. Designed by Sir Nigel Gresley, *Mallard* was part of a class of locomotives, the A4s, designed to pull fast express trains. *Mallard* is preserved today in Britain's National Railway Museum.

Sleek machine
For his A4s, Gresley designed a streamlined casing. Inspired by racing cars, the casing reduced air resistance and helped the locos reach high speeds.

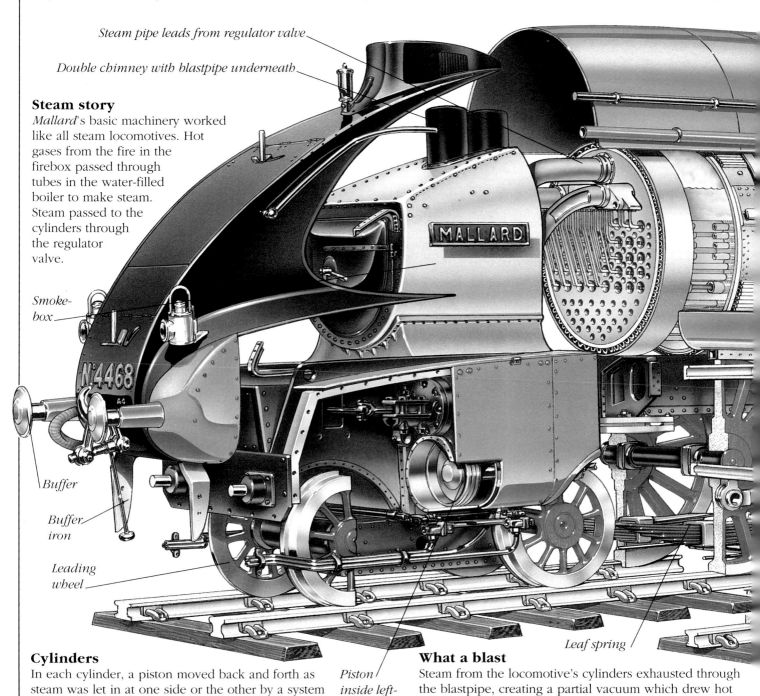

Steam pipe leads from regulator valve

Double chimney with blastpipe underneath

Steam story
Mallard's basic machinery worked like all steam locomotives. Hot gases from the fire in the firebox passed through tubes in the water-filled boiler to make steam. Steam passed to the cylinders through the regulator valve.

Smoke-box

Buffer

Buffer iron

Leading wheel

Leaf spring

Cylinders
In each cylinder, a piston moved back and forth as steam was let in at one side or the other by a system of valves. The back-and-forth action of each piston drove the wheels through the driving rods.

Piston inside left-hand cylinder

What a blast
Steam from the locomotive's cylinders exhausted through the blastpipe, creating a partial vacuum which drew hot gases along the boiler tubes and up the chimney. This also drew air into the firebox and made the fire burn hotter.

TECHNICAL DATA

WIDTH OVER FOOTPLATE: 2.7 M (9 FT)

HEIGHT: 3.98 M (13 FT 1 IN)

WEIGHT: 67,060 KG (147,840 LB)

MAXIMUM SPEED: 202 KM/H (126 MPH)

LENGTH WITH TENDER: 21.6 M (71 FT)

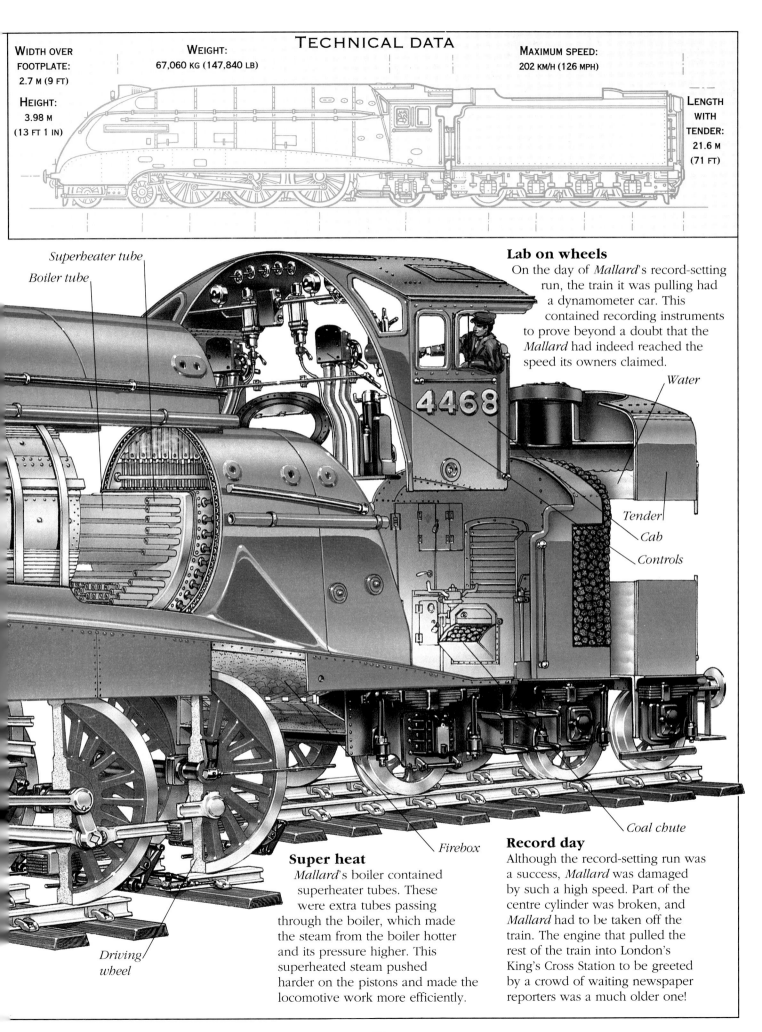

Superheater tube

Boiler tube

Driving wheel

Firebox

Coal chute

Water

Tender

Cab

Controls

4468

Lab on wheels
On the day of *Mallard*'s record-setting run, the train it was pulling had a dynamometer car. This contained recording instruments to prove beyond a doubt that the *Mallard* had indeed reached the speed its owners claimed.

Super heat
Mallard's boiler contained superheater tubes. These were extra tubes passing through the boiler, which made the steam from the boiler hotter and its pressure higher. This superheated steam pushed harder on the pistons and made the locomotive work more efficiently.

Record day
Although the record-setting run was a success, *Mallard* was damaged by such a high speed. Part of the centre cylinder was broken, and *Mallard* had to be taken off the train. The engine that pulled the rest of the train into London's King's Cross Station to be greeted by a crowd of waiting newspaper reporters was a much older one!

17

TURBINIA

IN JUNE 1897 THE WORLD'S BIGGEST NAVY WAS
putting on a show at Spithead, England to celebrate Queen Victoria's Diamond Jubilee. Lines of warships, the pride of the British Royal Navy, were smartly lined up for a review watched by representatives from around the world. Suddenly a small private boat appeared and sped up and down the lines. The onlookers were amazed as they watched the fastest boat in the world. The boat was the *Turbinia*, built by Charles Parsons to show his new invention, the steam turbine marine engine. His brilliant sales demonstration that day changed the world of shipping forever.

The new design
In Parsons' engine a coal-fired boiler heated water to make steam. The steam was forced through blades fitted round a shaft with a propeller on the end. The blades spun round, turning the shaft and the propeller. The new turbine engine was lighter, more efficient, and quieter than older types of steam engines.

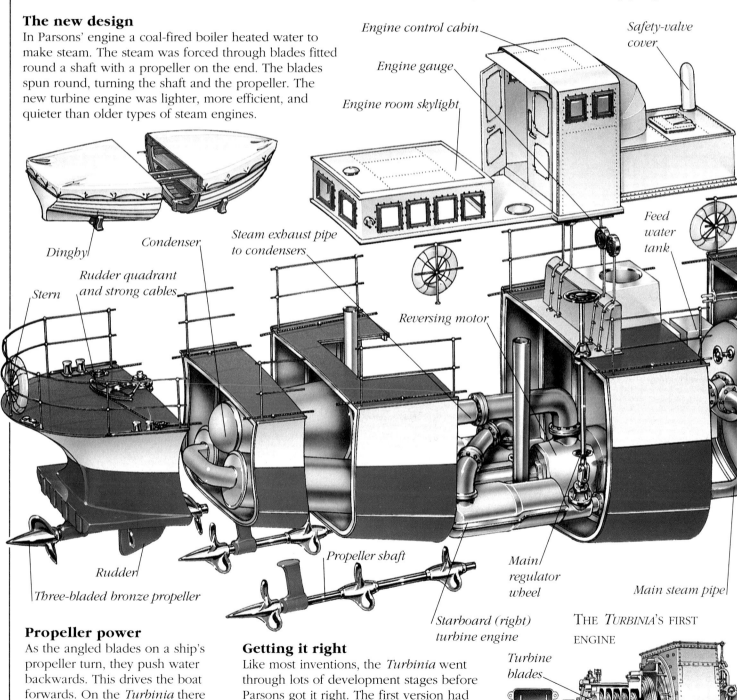

Engine control cabin

Safety-valve cover

Engine gauge

Engine room skylight

Feed water tank

Dinghy

Condenser

Steam exhaust pipe to condensers

Reversing motor

Stern

Rudder quadrant and strong cables

Rudder

Three-bladed bronze propeller

Propeller shaft

Main regulator wheel

Starboard (right) turbine engine

Main steam pipe

THE *TURBINIA*'S FIRST ENGINE

Turbine blades

Propeller power
As the angled blades on a ship's propeller turn, they push water backwards. This drives the boat forwards. On the *Turbinia* there were three turbines driving three separate shafts. Each shaft had three propellers fitted to it. The boat's top speed was 34.5 knots.

Getting it right
Like most inventions, the *Turbinia* went through lots of development stages before Parsons got it right. The first version had one turbine attached to a single propeller. However, this was incapable of the speeds Parsons had in mind. The final version (shown above) had three turbines.

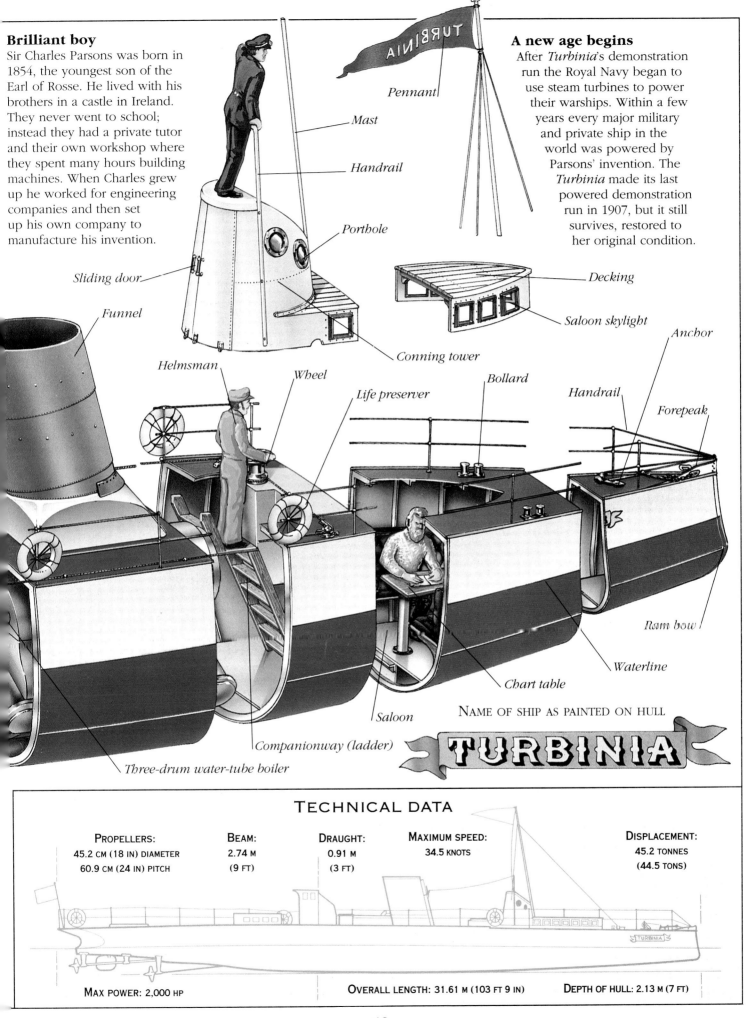

Brilliant boy

Sir Charles Parsons was born in 1854, the youngest son of the Earl of Rosse. He lived with his brothers in a castle in Ireland. They never went to school; instead they had a private tutor and their own workshop where they spent many hours building machines. When Charles grew up he worked for engineering companies and then set up his own company to manufacture his invention.

A new age begins

After *Turbinia*'s demonstration run the Royal Navy began to use steam turbines to power their warships. Within a few years every major military and private ship in the world was powered by Parsons' invention. The *Turbinia* made its last powered demonstration run in 1907, but it still survives, restored to her original condition.

Pennant

Mast

Handrail

Porthole

Sliding door

Funnel

Conning tower

Decking

Saloon skylight

Anchor

Helmsman

Wheel

Life preserver

Bollard

Handrail

Forepeak

Ram bow

Waterline

Chart table

Name of ship as painted on hull

Saloon

Companionway (ladder)

Three-drum water-tube boiler

TURBINIA

TECHNICAL DATA

PROPELLERS:	BEAM:	DRAUGHT:	MAXIMUM SPEED:	DISPLACEMENT:
45.2 CM (18 IN) DIAMETER	2.74 M	0.91 M	34.5 KNOTS	45.2 TONNES
60.9 CM (24 IN) PITCH	(9 FT)	(3 FT)		(44.5 TONS)

MAX POWER: 2,000 HP

OVERALL LENGTH: 31.61 M (103 FT 9 IN)

DEPTH OF HULL: 2.13 M (7 FT)

DRAG BIKE

FOR SHEER EXCITEMENT AND DANGER, MOTORCYCLE DRAG RACING IS one of the ultimate experiences! With very little protection the riders sit astride their super-charged monster machines knowing that one small error could prove disastrous. Once drag bikes raced against drag cars, but now drag bikes race in pairs over a 402 m (1,320 ft) straight course at speeds of nearly 325 km/h (200 mph). The riders need practice, planning, skill, and above all courage to explore the limits of their bikes' performance.

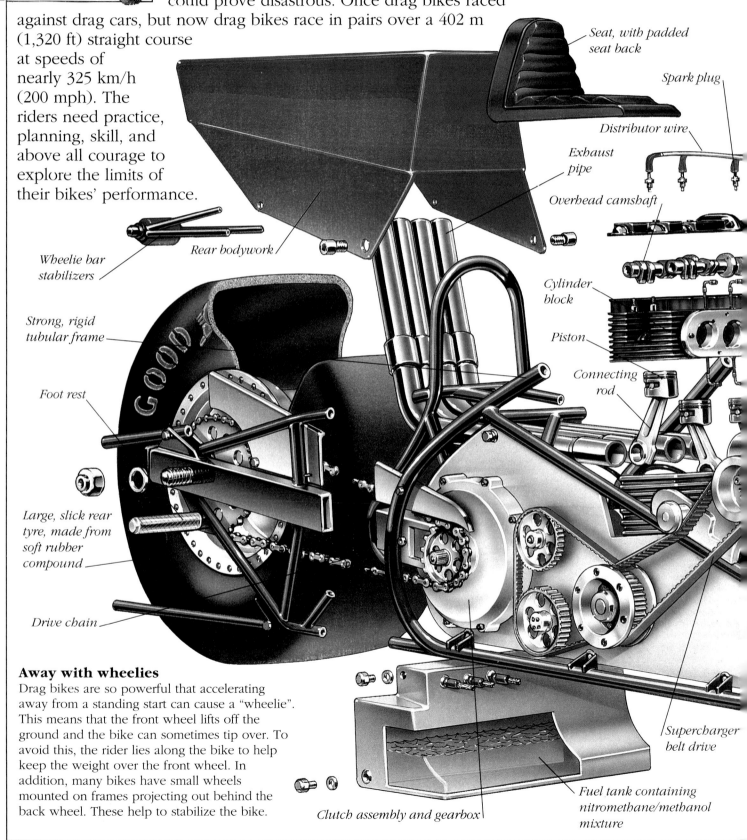

Seat, with padded seat back

Spark plug

Distributor wire

Exhaust pipe

Overhead camshaft

Cylinder block

Piston

Connecting rod

Rear bodywork

Wheelie bar stabilizers

Strong, rigid tubular frame

Foot rest

Large, slick rear tyre, made from soft rubber compound

Drive chain

Supercharger belt drive

Fuel tank containing nitromethane/methanol mixture

Clutch assembly and gearbox

Away with wheelies

Drag bikes are so powerful that accelerating away from a standing start can cause a "wheelie". This means that the front wheel lifts off the ground and the bike can sometimes tip over. To avoid this, the rider lies along the bike to help keep the weight over the front wheel. In addition, many bikes have small wheels mounted on frames projecting out behind the back wheel. These help to stabilize the bike.

Bare essentials

The essential drag bike is basically a frame, an engine, a seat, and two wheels! In addition, streamlined fairings are fitted over the front of the bike and also on to the front of the frame underneath. The fairings cut down wind resistance and help the bikes to reach very high speeds during a race.

TECHNICAL DATA

GROUND CLEARANCE:
7.5 CM
(3 IN)

ENGINE:
4-CYLINDER
1,000 CC

MAXIMUM SPEED:
200 MPH
(325 KM/H)

OVERALL LENGTH: 3 M (10 FT)

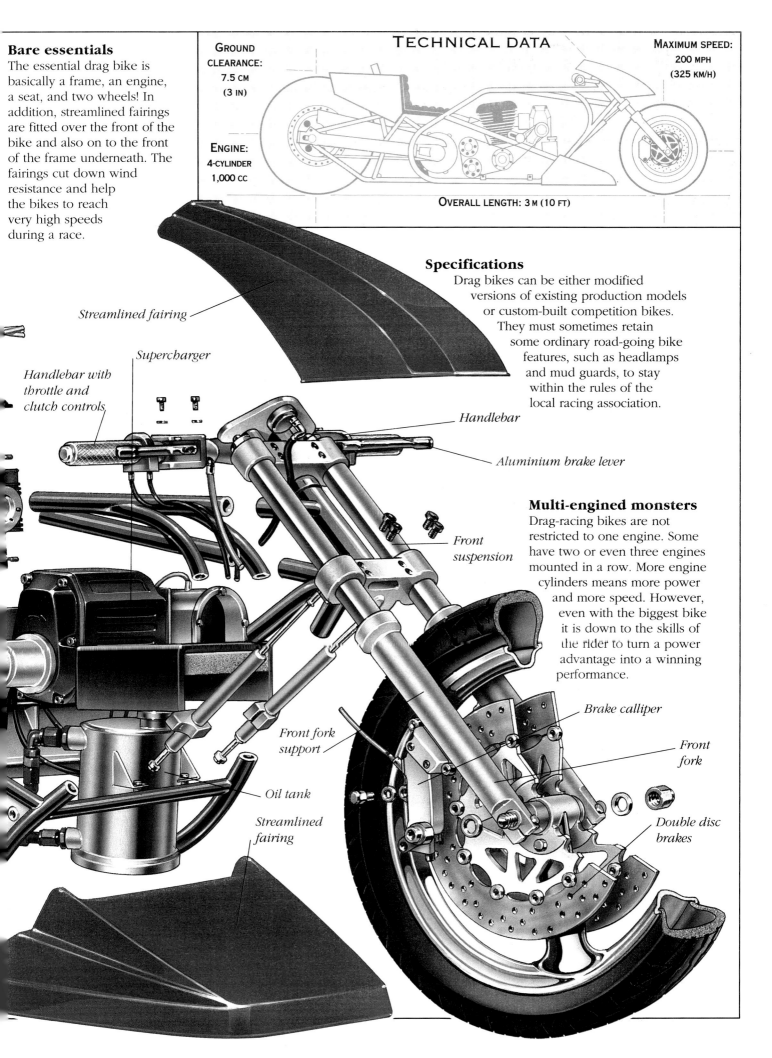

Streamlined fairing

Supercharger

Handlebar with throttle and clutch controls

Handlebar

Aluminium brake lever

Front suspension

Front fork support

Oil tank

Streamlined fairing

Brake calliper

Front fork

Double disc brakes

Specifications

Drag bikes can be either modified versions of existing production models or custom-built competition bikes. They must sometimes retain some ordinary road-going bike features, such as headlamps and mud guards, to stay within the rules of the local racing association.

Multi-engined monsters

Drag-racing bikes are not restricted to one engine. Some have two or even three engines mounted in a row. More engine cylinders means more power and more speed. However, even with the biggest bike it is down to the skills of the rider to turn a power advantage into a winning performance.

POWERBOAT

OFFSHORE POWERBOATS ARE THE SLEEK monsters of watersport. They race over the open sea on courses which can be up to 257 km (160 miles) long. Some are mono-hulled (with one hull) and some (like the boat shown here) are catamarans, which means they have two narrow parallel hulls. They bounce over the ocean surface at speeds of well over 160 km/h (100 mph). Powerboat racing is not for the timid. The boat frame and crew must be strong enough to endure fierce and constant battering during a race.

Exhaust pipe

V-12 Lamborghini engine

Thirsty work

Racing powerboats use either inboard or outboard engines. An outboard engine is one attached and hinged on to the back of the boat. The craft shown here has two V-12 Lamborghini engines mounted inboard, which means they are positioned inside the boat's frame. These engines are very powerful and also very thirsty. They can use 181 l (40 gal) of fuel per hour when racing!

Transom takes the force of the pushing propellers

Engine exhaust outlets

Streamlined cowling

Hydraulic ram steers boat

Trim flap controls angle of boat in water

Fuel tank

TECHNICAL DATA

PROPULSION:
SURFACE DRIVE
WAVE-PIERCING PROPELLER

CONSTRUCTION:
ALUMINIUM SHEET ON WELDED ALUMINIUM FRAME

ENGINES:
2 x V-12 LAMBORGHINI 8.2 LITRE
950 HP EACH

LENGTH:
15.2 M (50 FT)

In the cockpit

Boats of this size usually need two crew members to control them. In this catamaran the driver sits in front with the throttle operator behind. The cockpit is surrounded by a clear canopy that helps to streamline the boat and gives the crew a wide field of vision. It is based on a US F-16 jet fighter canopy, with the modification of an escape hole in the top in case of an emergency.

The kill switch

As part of race regulations each crew member must wear a "kill-switch" cord attached to one wrist. If they are thrown out of the boat the kill-switch cord will automatically stop the engine, so that the boat does not veer across the ocean out of control.

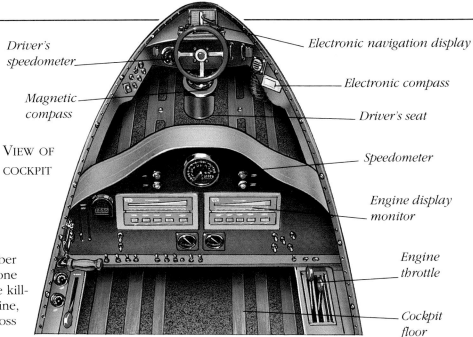

VIEW OF COCKPIT

Driver's speedometer

Magnetic compass

Electronic navigation display

Electronic compass

Driver's seat

Speedometer

Engine display monitor

Engine throttle

Cockpit floor

At the controls

The driver keeps the boat on the right course with the help of electronic satellite navigation systems. They indicate very precisely the boat's position. The other crew member controls the engine speed and trim. This means that if the nose is too high the trim flaps can be moved to bring it down. It's even possible to pump fuel between the fuel tanks to keep one side level with the other.

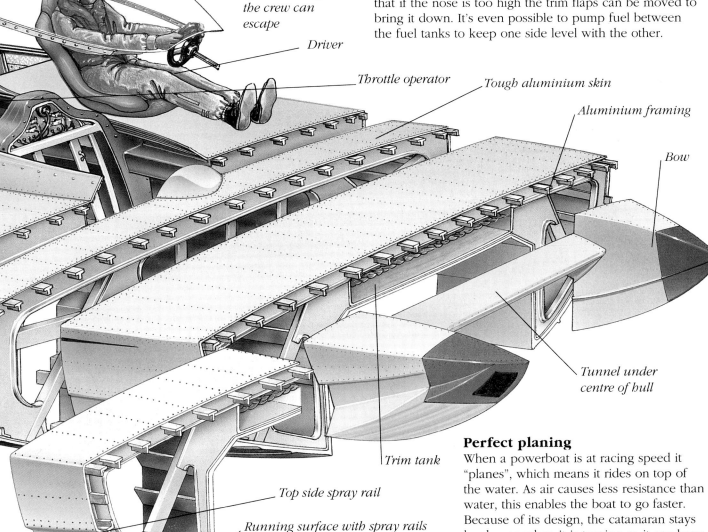

Safety harness

Protective canopy open at the top so the crew can escape

Driver

Throttle operator

Tough aluminium skin

Aluminium framing

Bow

Tunnel under centre of hull

Trim tank

Top side spray rail

Running surface with spray rails

Perfect planing

When a powerboat is at racing speed it "planes", which means it rides on top of the water. As air causes less resistance than water, this enables the boat to go faster. Because of its design, the catamaran stays level even when it is turning so it can keep up its speed, riding on the air cushion.

TEMPEST V

IT IS JUNE 1944 AND A PILOT OF BRITAIN'S ROYAL AIR FORCE is straining his eyes trying to penetrate the darkness of the night sky. He is not looking for an enemy aeroplane, but an unmanned V-1 rocket, a deadly jet-powered "flying bomb". Suddenly the pilot sees the V-1's jet exhaust as a glimmer of light in the distance. The Hawker Tempest V aircraft he is flying is one of the fastest propeller-driven aeroplanes. Flying behind the bomb, he lines the exhaust up in his gunsight and fires, then turns quickly away as the V-1 explodes.

High, fast, and deadly

V-1 flying bombs flew at an altitude of between 450-600 m (1,500-2,000 ft). They were packed with explosives to wreak havoc when they fell to earth and blew up. The Hawker Tempests were among the fastest propeller-powered planes of their day, fast enough to catch the bombs as they sped on their deadly journey.

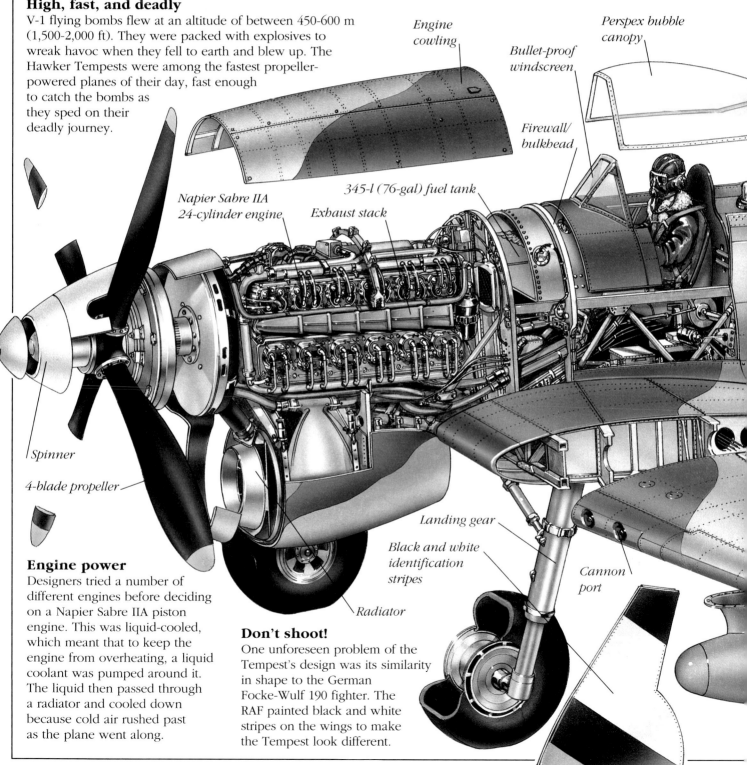

Engine cowling

Perspex bubble canopy

Bullet-proof windscreen

Firewall/ bulkhead

345-l (76-gal) fuel tank

Napier Sabre IIA 24-cylinder engine

Exhaust stack

Spinner

4-blade propeller

Landing gear

Black and white identification stripes

Cannon port

Radiator

Engine power

Designers tried a number of different engines before deciding on a Napier Sabre IIA piston engine. This was liquid-cooled, which meant that to keep the engine from overheating, a liquid coolant was pumped around it. The liquid then passed through a radiator and cooled down because cold air rushed past as the plane went along.

Don't shoot!

One unforeseen problem of the Tempest's design was its similarity in shape to the German Focke-Wulf 190 fighter. The RAF painted black and white stripes on the wings to make the Tempest look different.

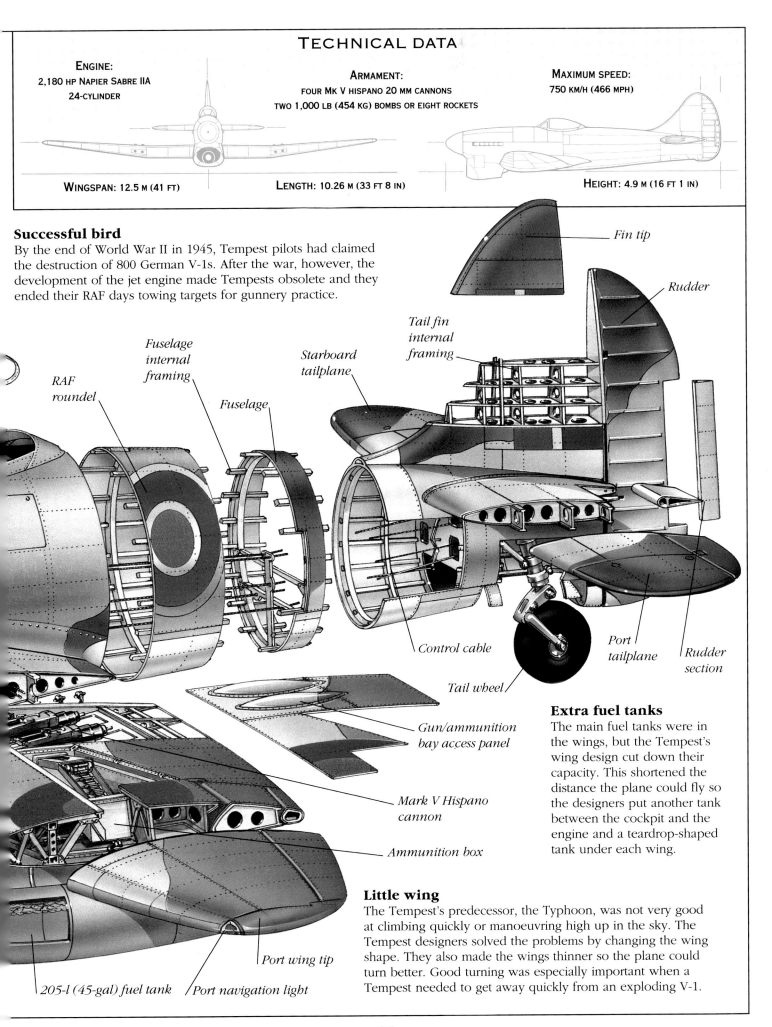

ENGINE:
2,180 HP NAPIER SABRE IIA
24-CYLINDER

ARMAMENT:
FOUR MK V HISPANO 20 MM CANNONS
TWO 1,000 LB (454 KG) BOMBS OR EIGHT ROCKETS

MAXIMUM SPEED:
750 KM/H (466 MPH)

WINGSPAN: 12.5 M (41 FT)

LENGTH: 10.26 M (33 FT 8 IN)

HEIGHT: 4.9 M (16 FT 1 IN)

Successful bird

By the end of World War II in 1945, Tempest pilots had claimed the destruction of 800 German V-1s. After the war, however, the development of the jet engine made Tempests obsolete and they ended their RAF days towing targets for gunnery practice.

Fin tip

Rudder

Tail fin internal framing

Fuselage internal framing

Starboard tailplane

RAF roundel

Fuselage

Control cable

Tail wheel

Port tailplane

Rudder section

Gun/ammunition bay access panel

Mark V Hispano cannon

Ammunition box

Extra fuel tanks

The main fuel tanks were in the wings, but the Tempest's wing design cut down their capacity. This shortened the distance the plane could fly so the designers put another tank between the cockpit and the engine and a teardrop-shaped tank under each wing.

Little wing

The Tempest's predecessor, the Typhoon, was not very good at climbing quickly or manoeuvring high up in the sky. The Tempest designers solved the problems by changing the wing shape. They also made the wings thinner so the plane could turn better. Good turning was especially important when a Tempest needed to get away quickly from an exploding V-1.

205-l (45-gal) fuel tank

Port wing tip

Port navigation light

INDY CAR

INDY CAR RACING BEGAN IN THE UNITED STATES EARLY in the 1900s. It takes its name from the city of Indianapolis, Indiana, where a new speedway track was first used for racing in 1909. Today, Indy car racing is one of the most popular motorsports. The Indy car is heavier than the other well-known racing car, the Formula 1, and has a turbocharged engine which increases the power output. Add to this aerodynamic features that hold the car to the track and you have an amazing machine well able to achieve the speeds of 322 km/h (200 mph) reached in an Indy car race.

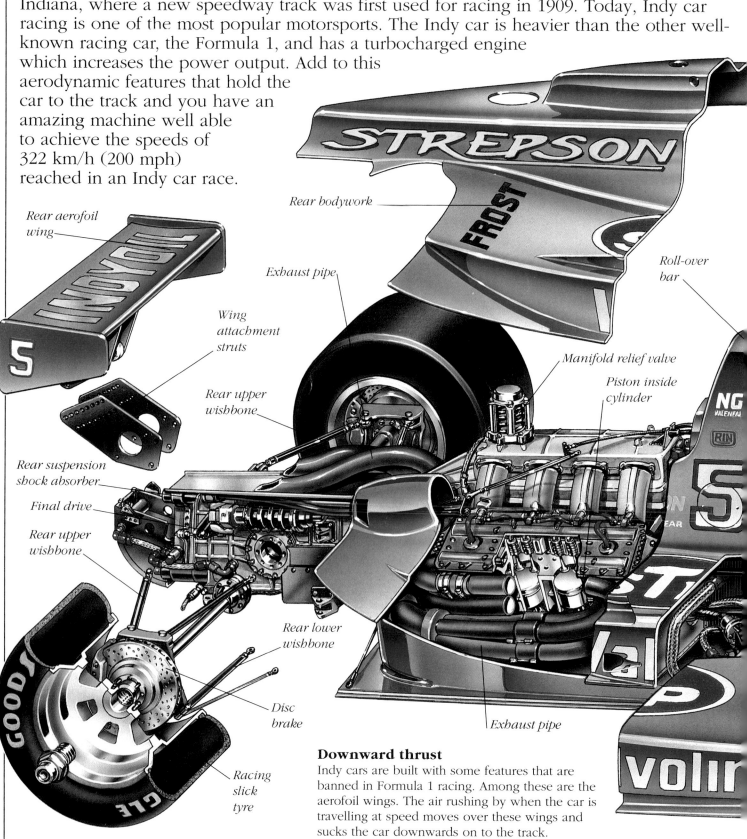

Rear aerofoil wing

Rear bodywork

Roll-over bar

Exhaust pipe

Wing attachment struts

Rear upper wishbone

Manifold relief valve

Piston inside cylinder

Rear suspension shock absorber

Final drive

Rear upper wishbone

Rear lower wishbone

Disc brake

Exhaust pipe

Racing slick tyre

Downward thrust
Indy cars are built with some features that are banned in Formula 1 racing. Among these are the aerofoil wings. The air rushing by when the car is travelling at speed moves over these wings and sucks the car downwards on to the track.

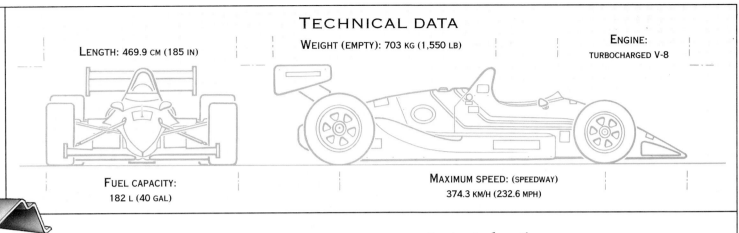

TECHNICAL DATA

LENGTH: 469.9 CM (185 IN)

WEIGHT (EMPTY): 703 KG (1,550 LB)

ENGINE: TURBOCHARGED V-8

FUEL CAPACITY: 182 L (40 GAL)

MAXIMUM SPEED: (SPEEDWAY) 374.3 KM/H (232.6 MPH)

Survival

The Indy car cockpit is made of carbon-fibre to withstand impact and provide maximum protection for the driver in the event of a crash. The roll-over bar provides protection for the driver's head.

Instant elevation

Indy cars are specially built to cope with the banking (elevation on the outside) of the oval track. At the flick of a switch an Indy car driver can elevate the right side of the car using compressed air, to compensate for the elevation.

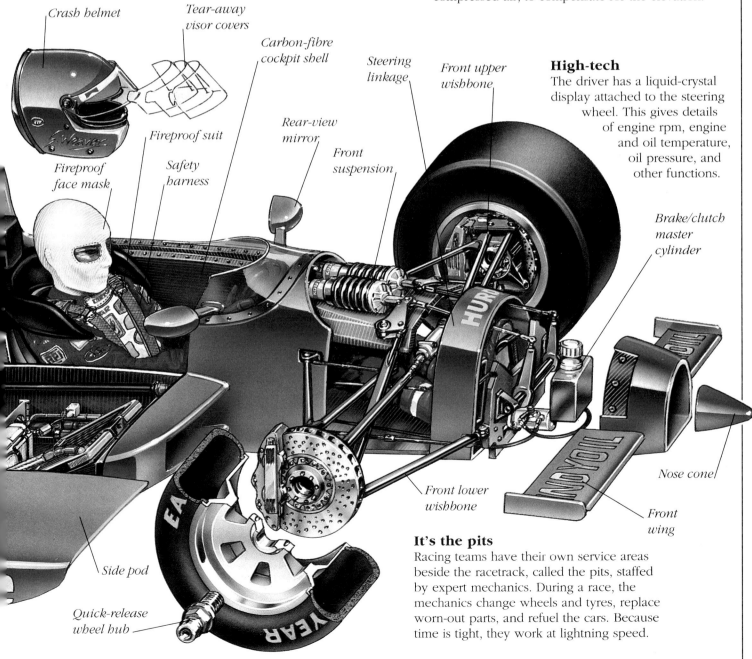

Crash helmet

Tear-away visor covers

Carbon-fibre cockpit shell

Steering linkage

Front upper wishbone

Rear-view mirror

Front suspension

Fireproof suit

Safety harness

Fireproof face mask

Front lower wishbone

Side pod

Quick-release wheel hub

Brake/clutch master cylinder

Nose cone

Front wing

High-tech

The driver has a liquid-crystal display attached to the steering wheel. This gives details of engine rpm, engine and oil temperature, oil pressure, and other functions.

It's the pits

Racing teams have their own service areas beside the racetrack, called the pits, staffed by expert mechanics. During a race, the mechanics change wheels and tyres, replace worn-out parts, and refuel the cars. Because time is tight, they work at lightning speed.

SPEEDLINE

DURING THE LAST 150 YEARS, humans have reached ever-higher speeds in cars, trains, boats, and aircraft. People were afraid to travel in the first cars because of their speed, yet now many people fly in airliners going faster than the speed of sound. Here are some speed machine milestones.

1885 BENZ TRICYCLE 12-16 KM/H (8-10 MPH)

1860s TEA CLIPPER 20 KM/H (12 MPH)

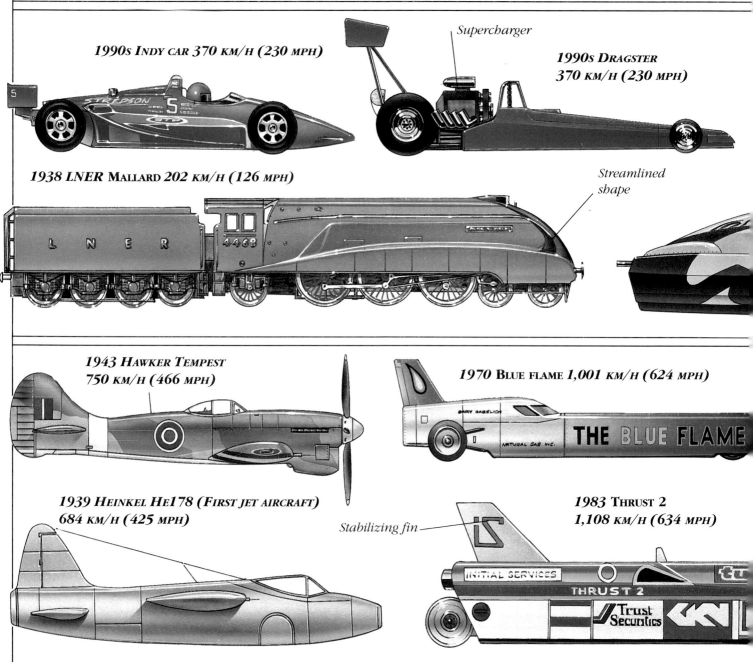

1990s INDY CAR 370 KM/H (230 MPH)

Supercharger

1990s DRAGSTER 370 KM/H (230 MPH)

1938 LNER MALLARD 202 KM/H (126 MPH)

Streamlined shape

1943 HAWKER TEMPEST 750 KM/H (466 MPH)

1970 BLUE FLAME 1,001 KM/H (624 MPH)

THE BLUE FLAME

1939 HEINKEL HE178 (FIRST JET AIRCRAFT) 684 KM/H (425 MPH)

Stabilizing fin

1983 THRUST 2 1,108 KM/H (634 MPH)

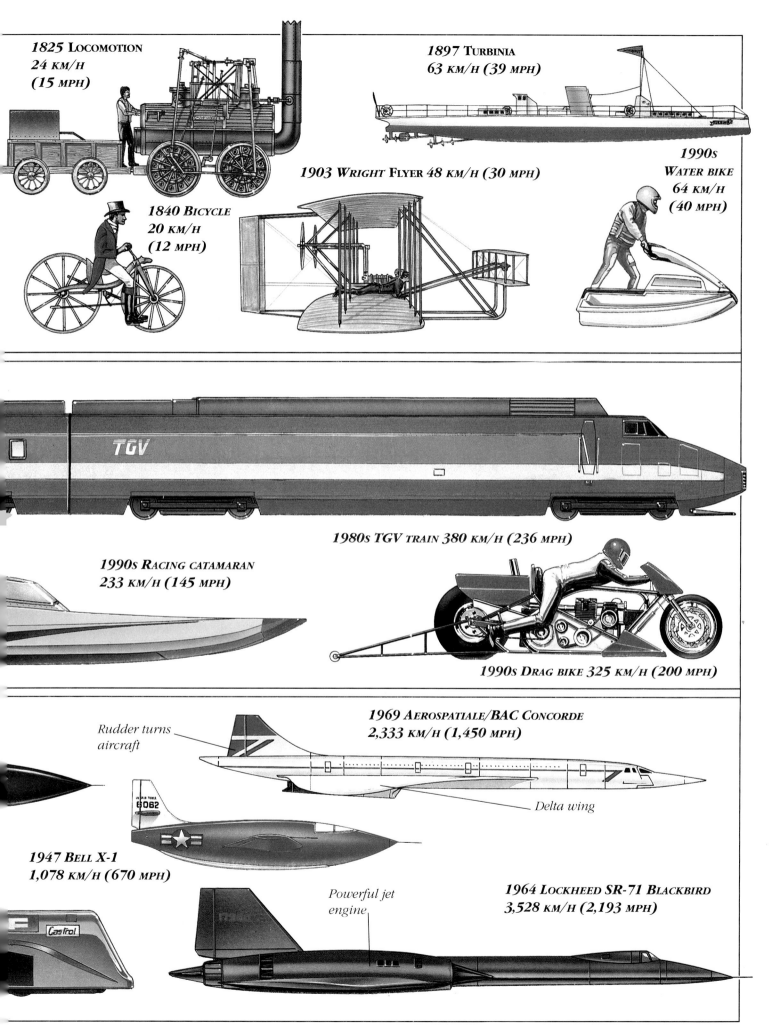

1825 LOCOMOTION
24 KM/H
(15 MPH)

1897 TURBINIA
63 KM/H (39 MPH)

1903 WRIGHT FLYER 48 KM/H (30 MPH)

1990s
WATER BIKE
64 KM/H
(40 MPH)

1840 BICYCLE
20 KM/H
(12 MPH)

1980s TGV TRAIN 380 KM/H (236 MPH)

1990s RACING CATAMARAN
233 KM/H (145 MPH)

1990s DRAG BIKE 325 KM/H (200 MPH)

1969 AEROSPATIALE/BAC CONCORDE
2,333 KM/H (1,450 MPH)

Rudder turns aircraft

Delta wing

1947 BELL X-1
1,078 KM/H (670 MPH)

Powerful jet engine

1964 LOCKHEED SR-71 BLACKBIRD
3,528 KM/H (2,193 MPH)

GLOSSARY

Acceleration
The rate at which a vehicle or a craft picks up speed.

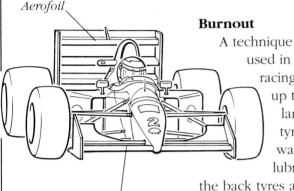

Aerofoil

Aerofoil

Aerofoil
A wing-like structure on a car or plane. As the vehicle travels along the aerofoil forces air more quickly over one side than the other, depending on its shape. This creates either lift (as with a plane) or downforce (as with a racing car).

Air-resistance
The pushing force exerted by air as an object moves through it. Speed machine designers try to keep this low so that it won't slow down a moving vehicle.

Ballast
Heavy material such as stone and iron used to steady a ship and make sure it sits evenly in the water, without leaning to one side or the other.

Boiler
The part of a steam engine in which the water is heated up to make steam.

Burnout
A technique used in drag racing to warm up the large rear tyres. Using water to lubricate them, the back tyres are spun while the vehicle is stationary. This cleans the tyres and heats the tyre rubber so it will grip the track better.

Catamaran
A boat with two parallel narrow hulls, one on either side. This cuts down on water resistance and helps the boat to go faster.

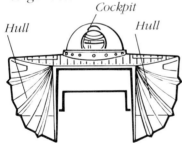

Hull *Cockpit* *Hull*

CATAMARAN

Cylinder
Part of an engine. It is a tubular chamber in which a piston is pushed in and out by the force of steam or hot gas entering the cylinder under pressure.

Disc brake
In this type of braking system brake pads clamp on to a disc attached to a vehicle wheel. The resulting friction slows the wheel down.

Elapsed time
The time taken by a drag car or a drag bike to complete a run of a quarter of a mile.

Exhaust
The waste gases expelled from the cylinders of an engine once fuel has been burnt in them.

Fuel tank
A chamber where fuel is kept. When a vehicle is started, fuel travels from the tank via pipes to the engine.

G-force
The action of gravity on the human body, normally measured as 1. The effect of manoeuvring in a high-speed craft can increase this measurement. For instance, a g-force of 8 (as experienced in a racing powerboat) means that the body weighs effectively eight times its normal weight.

Inboard
The term used when a powerboat engine is positioned inside the boat's frame.

Internal combustion engine
A type of engine which works by combusting (burning) fuel within metal cylinders inside the engine. Inside each cylinder a metal barrel called a piston is moved up or down by the forces caused by the burning hot gases. The motion of the piston powers other parts of the vehicle.

INTERNAL COMBUSTION ENGINE

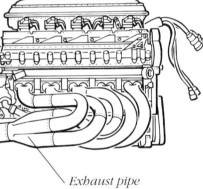

Exhaust pipe

Jet engine
An engine that produces a powerful jet of hot gas (as in a plane) or water (as in a PWC) to push a vehicle or craft along.

Nitromethane
A particularly rich fuel used in drag racing engines. It burns very efficiently, helping to increase the engine's power output.

Outboard
The term used when a powerboat engine is positioned outside the boat at the stern.

Piston

A metal barrel inside a cylinder. It is pushed up or down in the cylinder by forces caused by burning fuel (as in a combustion engine) or by oil pumped into the cylinder (as in a hydraulic system).

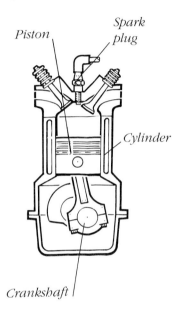

Piston

Spark plug

Cylinder

Crankshaft

CUTAWAY OF ENGINE

Personal watercraft

PWC for short. A kind of motorbike on water skis, used in watersports. One particular make of PWC is called a "Jet Ski".

PWC

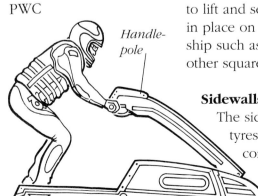

Handle-pole

Planing

The combined effect of speed and construction that allows boats to skim across the water's surface by raising them up on a very thin cushion of air. Air provides less resistance than water, so a boat can travel faster if it planes.

Propeller

A set of blades mounted on a spinning shaft. The spinning action creates forces that push a craft through air or water.

Radiator

Part of an engine cooling system. Heat generated by a working engine is drawn off by a coolant liquid which circulates around the engine. Heat passes out into the air as the coolant travels through the radiator. Then the cooled-down coolant flows back around the engine to do its job again.

Running rigging

A system of ropes used to lift and secure the sails in place on a sailing ship such as a clipper or other square-rigger.

Sidewalls

The side surfaces of tyres. They do not come into contact with the track surface.

Standing rigging

A system of ropes or wire cables used to hold the masts of a sailing ship firmly in place.

Streamlining

The smooth design of a speed machine, which enables it to move more quickly by keeping air or water resistance to a minimum as it travels along. Air or water resistance get higher if there are more flat surfaces to push against. They get lower if there is a smooth surface to travel round.

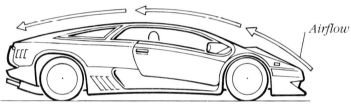

Airflow

STREAMLINING

Supercharger

This is sometimes called a blower. It is a device to help an engine produce more power by forcing a fuel vapour and air mixture into the engine under greatly increased pressure.

Supersonic

Faster than the speed of sound. Jet planes are now supersonic. Record-breaking supersonic landspeed vehicles are being designed.

Terminal velocity

The highest speed reached by a drag car or a drag bike during a run over a quarter-mile course.

Throttle

The device that controls the flow of fuel into an engine, causing it to either speed up or slow down.

Trim

The angle that a boat sits in the water.

Wheelie

As a result of accelerating very quickly on a motorbike, the front wheel rises and the bike performs a wheelie. The acceleration of drag bikes is so quick that many have "wheelie bars" behind the rear wheel to stop them flipping over.

WHEELIE

INDEX

Acknowledgements

Dorling Kindersley would like to thank the following people who helped in the preparation of this book:

Gary Biggin for additional line artwork
Lynn Bresler for the index
Cougar Marine
Kawasaki Motors (UK) Limited
Museum of British Road Transport, Coventry
Tyne and Wear Museums